JOKES
&
QUOTES
FOR SPEECHES

JOKES
&
QUOTES
FOR SPEECHES

PETER ELDIN

WARD LOCK

A WARD LOCK BOOK

First published in this edition in the UK in 1994 by Ward Lock
Villiers House, 41/47 Strand, London WC2N 5JE

A Cassell Imprint

Reprinted 1994

Distributed in the United States
by Sterling Publishing Co., Inc.
387 Park Avenue South, New York, NY 10016-8810

Distributed in Australia
by Capricorn Link (Australia) Pty Ltd
2/13 Carrington Road, Castle Hill, NSW 2154

British Library Cataloguing-in-Publication Data
A catalogue record for this book is available from the British Library

ISBN 0-7063-7270-0

Typeset by Data Forum Ltd, Grantham, Lincs.

Printed and bound in Great Britain by
Biddles Ltd, Guildford and King's Lynn

Contents

Introduction

In my work as a professional writer and entertainer I have frequently been called upon to make speeches at business lunches, professional organizations, ladies' groups, book promotions, school speech days, and so on, as well as being the subject of numerous interviews for newspapers, magazines, radio and television. As a family man I have also done my fair share of speeches at weddings, anniversaries, christenings and other family gatherings.

When I first started receiving invitations to speak my biggest problem was finding appropriate jokes and quotes to include in my speeches. To overcome this problem I began collecting jokes and quotes from all manner of sources. Some of these are included in this selection, which I hope you will find useful for any speeches you may be called upon to make.

Although this is intended as a book of reference rather than a book to read through from beginning to end, I suggest that you do just that. The book has been divided into sections but many of the jokes and quotations can be adapted for other situations.

If you are searching for material for a wedding speech, for example, do not just refer to the section on weddings and anniversaries. Suitable material can also be found in the section on birthdays. The same is also true of a speech for a retirement presentation. The section on general jokes and quotes would certainly be worth looking at for any type of speech, and even areas that have nothing to do with your subject may provide the spark that will lift your speech from predictable run-of-the-mill to something your audience will remember for a long time to come.

Making a speech

This is not a book on how to prepare and deliver a speech. Rather it is designed to be used as a fund of over 500 jokes and quotes on which you can draw to spice up a speech. But, for the sake of completeness, a few tips on preparation and presentation will not go amiss.

PREPARE EARLY

One of the most important rules, and one ignored by a great many people, is to prepare well in advance.

Even if you are an expert on a subject you will not give of your best if you try to talk off the cuff. As soon as you know you are going to give a speech, start to work on it.

OBTAINING MATERIAL

If you are to make a speech on a particular subject your own knowledge of that subject will provide your first source of information. Get a large sheet of paper and note down everything you can think of that will be relevant to your speech.

Books are the next obvious source of material. If the subject is one in which you already have some interest and knowledge then you will probably have all the books you need. If not, the staff at your local public library will probably be only too willing to help you in your search.

Once you attune your mind to a particular subject you will find references leaping at you from newspapers, television and casual conversations. Carry a notebook with you at all times so you can jot down any bits of information or ideas. It is amazing how easy it is to forget an interesting snippet if you do not make a note of it immediately. Do not say 'I will make a note of that when I get home.' Do it straight away.

If you have to make a particularly long speech you will find it worthwhile keeping a small record card for each main point. On this card you can note down the subsidiary points, anecdotes and quotes as they come to you. Cards have the advantage that they can be rearranged into whatever order you wish without the need for copying everything out.

If your notes are neat (mine seldom are) they can be used as an *aide memoire* when delivering the speech. My notes tend to end up with so much material on them that I have to cut a lot out. This means re-writing the main points again at a later stage for my 'cue card(s)'. A word processor is invaluable if you have to do a lot of rewriting.

If you do your research thoroughly you will end up with far too much material for your needs. That is a good thing. It is much easier to discard something you do not need than to create a half hour speech from ten minutes worth of information.

KEEP IT SIMPLE

It is not necessary to tell your audience everything you know, or have discovered, about the subject. That would be boring – and if they were at all interested they could have looked it up for themselves.

Rather than relate the whole spectrum of a subject, try to pick just one aspect as the focal point for your speech.

Don't try to be clever. You are speaking to entertain and inform your audience – not to prove you are better than they are. Keep your speech simple and use only words you would normally use. If you try to impress your audience with your superior intellect you will succeed only in making yourself sound a fool.

STARTING AND FINISHING

Pay particular attention to the beginning and end of your speech. Your opening remarks set both the tone of your speech and the reaction you will get from your audience. The closing remarks round off the speech and bring your talk to a definite end.

I do not advocate memorizing a speech word for word but the opening and closing remarks are exceptions to this rule. If you memorize your opening comments you start without hesitation and this will give you confidence in your performance. Similarly, a memorized closing remark rounds off the speech and provides the cue for applause.

When I was a young amateur magician a professional once told me 'Start well and finish well; and you can put what you like in the middle.' Whilst I do not agree with this entirely it is certainly a good rule of thumb for speeches, as well as for a variety act.

KEEP IT SHORT

Another piece of advice for a variety act, which applies equally to a speech is, 'leave 'em asking for more'. In other words, do not go on for too long and outstay your welcome.

Whatever you do, do not speak for too long. Remember the old adage, 'stand up, speak up, then shut up'. It is advice that all speakers would do well to remember.

In my notes I have a short verse credited to R. Cheney which emphasizes the need for brevity:

Charm and wit and levity
May help you at the start
But at the end, it's brevity
That wins the public's heart.

CONSIDER YOUR AUDIENCE

It is important to bear in mind the type of audience you will have and to slant your material towards them. The same is also true of the occasion – no-one wants a humorous speech at a funeral!

I well remember an occasion many years ago when I was invited to talk to a professional organization (which, to save my embarrassment, shall be nameless). I decided that, as all the other speeches of the day would be dry, dull and eminently serious, I would give a humorous speech. If I had done some research beforehand I would have discovered the type of speech they expected and constructed mine accordingly. As it was, I misjudged the situation entirely and the speech 'died a death'. A dry, dusty approach was what had been expected.

I have used a similar technique when I have been invited to school speech days. Nearly all the speeches are dry and dusty so a humorous speech goes down well. However, as I have written a number of successful books for children I know my audience and therein lies the secret of success for any speech. You must judge your audience and construct your speech accordingly.

MEMORY VERSUS NOTES

Never try to memorize your speech word for word. If you forget just one little thing it will affect the rest of your speech. You will start worrying about the ommission, more lines will get forgotten, the structure you have so carefully defined will start to crumble and you may well end up as a gibbering incoherent jelly.

On the other hand I personally do not recommend reading a speech. It would be easier to run off sufficient copies and hand one to each member of your audience so they can read it at their leisure.

In most cases you will find that the best approach lies between the two extremes. That is, to have notes of the salient points you wish to make. If you have built up your speech by jotting down notes and ideas you will have these points outlined already. Notes should be succinct enough that you can take each point in at a glance but sufficiently full so you understand what they mean.

There is no hard and fast rule as to extent and layout of your notes. You are the one who has got to use them so prepare them according to your own requirements.

Highlighter pens can be useful in accentuating particular items in your notes.

As you look down at your notes you will see the next point to be mentioned and this should remind you of what you want to say. Provided you get your points across it does not really matter if you then forget a joke or a quote which you had originally intended to include.

Cue words or phrases to remind you of the jokes can be added to the card if you wish. Just the tag line of a joke should prove a sufficient guide.

If you are making any direct quotes then it is a good idea to write them out in full and refer to them openly so you can quote word for word.

Do not try to hide your notes. Unless you are supposed to be speaking entirely off the cuff people will know you have prepared for your speech and any use of notes is regarded as acceptable.

When I am called upon to speak I always use cue cards. These are standard 5 by 3 inch record cards. I always number the cards in sequence just in case I should drop them. It hasn't happened yet but I find it is as well to be prepared for all eventualities.

Apart from impromptu speeches the only time I have not used such cards was when I was asked to address a group of businessmen. On that occasion the use of a card was inappropriate for the subject of my talk was memory improvement!

REHEARSE YOUR SPEECH

If you have a tape recorder record your speech and then play it back. You may be surprised at what you hear. You will almost certainly find several areas in which an improvement can be made.

If you have a video camera, better still. Position it so it films the whole upper half of your body. Now go into your speech and play it back afterwards. You may well be surprised at some of the disconcerting habits you have. Try to look at the video from a stranger's viewpoint. And then start working on getting rid of those irritating habits and developing a better stance, better mannerisms and all-round better presentation.

All performers rehearse and in giving a speech you take on the role of a performer. So you should rehearse your speech as much as possible. Rehearse out loud and try to visualize your audience before you as you do so.

As you rehearse, repeatedly tell yourself that the speech will go down well. Really believe it and your subconscious mind will work on this positive suggestion so that your belief will become reality when you take the stage.

Just for one moment imagine your speech will be a failure and it almost certainly will be. Think positively and you will deliver a successful speech.

ENJOY YOURSELF!

Above all you must enjoy giving your speech. If you are apprehensive this will be conveyed to your listeners. Think of everyone in your audience as your friend and try to speak to each one in turn by making eye contact with different people around the room as you speak.

If you are comfortable, relaxed, fully rehearsed and enjoy making the speech then the audience will enjoy it as well.

USING JOKES AND QUOTES

On the pages that follow there is a wide range of material suitable for an immense variety of situations. It is important that you choose your material carefully. Everything you say should be in keeping with your own character, the tone of your speech and the type of audience you are addressing.

While it is useful to include some quips or quotes in your speech try not to overdo it. It is easy to compile a speech of never-ending jokes using this book but it is not a good idea to do this. If you do your speech will have no impact whatsoever.

Remember the purpose of your speech. If you

have been invited to give thanks to someone, to present some prizes, to launch a product, or to announce an anniversary then that is what you should do. Keep the purpose of your speech in mind at all times and be careful not to include jokes, quotes, or other material just for the sake of it.

Your audience should be entertained by your speech but that does not mean you should become a stand-up comedian – if your audience wanted to listen to a comedian they would have hired one or stayed at home and watched the television.

ADAPTING MATERIAL

Much of the material in this book can be adapted to suit different occasions.

Take, for example, the golfing joke on page 53. For an 'At Work' situation it could be re-worded along the lines of: 'I don't work at Smith Brothers any more.' said Mike Smogsbourn. 'Why not?' asked Fred 'I thought you got on well with your boss.' 'No.' said Mike. Would you work with someone who took three-hour lunch breaks, came in drunk every day and made a mess of every order he handled?' Fred admitted that he wouldn't. 'Neither would my boss.' said Mike.

For a matrimonial situation it could be 'My wife and I have parted.' etc.

'Would you live with someone who . . . . .'

'Neither would my wife.'

A useful way to adapt jokes is to use the names of your friends instead of Mike Smogsbourn, or whatever. Provided you do not use this approach with jokes that could be harmful or offensive it can be effective to personalize a remark if you can.

So, instead of saying 'he' use the name of someone your audience knows. Instead of saying 'a street' use the name of a local street. Instead of saying 'a shop' use the name of a local store.

It is much more interesting, if instead of saying something like:

'A man booked into a hotel . . .' you say

'Peter Eldin booked into the Savoy . . .'

Even some of the quotations can be adapted with a little thought. Take the quote by W.C. Fields on page 42. This is itself an adaptation of the old saying 'If at first you don't succeed try, try, try, again.'

By giving it some thought you could come up with something like:

Advice to drunks: 'If at first you don't succeed try, try, try a gin.'

Advice to lovers: 'If at first you don't succeed try a little ardour.'

Advice to someone who wants to commit suicide: 'If at first you don't succeed try, try a gun.'

'If at first you don't succeed give the job to someone else.'

'If at first you don't succeed it could be because you've got the instructions upside down.'

Most remarks can be changed to lift your speech out of the ordinary, provided you are prepared to give some thought to the subject.

Christenings and birthdays

As a general rule speeches for christenings and birthdays should be happy and light.

To my mind they should be impromptu – or at least appear to be so.

Possibly the safest form of speech on such occasions is a simple but sincere toast to the person whose birthday or christening it is: 'May he (or she) enjoy long life, health, wealth and happiness.'

Even if you have no intention of speaking it does no harm to do some advance preparation if there is any likelihood of your being asked to say a few words.

If you are not called upon your ego may be slightly dented but the speech preparation will not go amiss. Keep the speech in hand for some future occasion. It may even turn out to be a better speech in the long run for you will have more time to polish it to perfection.

JOKES

As my wife tucks our youngster into bed each night she always says 'Darling, if there is anything you want during the night, just call Mummy – and I'll send Daddy in.'

There is only one way I can make my kids notice that I've got home from the office – I walk in front of the television set.

The other night I read my young son a bedtime story. When I'd finished he said 'That was quite good, Dad. But not so good as the story you told Mum about working late at the office.'

When my son's class were due to start sex education classes the school asked for written permission from a parent for each pupil to attend. My wife wrote to the teacher. 'Yes, my son has my permission to take sex education – mentally.'

A three-year-old child gets more fun from the cardboard box than from the expensive present it contained.

How times have changed. In my day you would hear boys boasting, 'My Dad is better than your Dad.' Nowadays they say, 'My computer is better than your computer.'

A little boy asked his father how he was born so the father explained that daddies planted seeds in mummies and then babies grew.
The young boy digested this for a moment and then asked, 'Was my picture on the packet?'

Children are the ups and downs of life. They get you down all day and keep you up all night.

Some friends of mine are expecting their fifth child. They are rather worried about it because someone told them that one in every five children is Chinese.

When I was a baby I always dreaded my father changing my nappy. He used to be a hand grenade instructor and could never forget the fact. Out of habit he would pull out the pin, count to five, and then throw me as far as he could.

When my brother was born my sister said to Mum,

'He's not very pretty, is he? No wonder you hid him under your dress all that time.'

A woman took her daughter and a friend to the zoo. When they came to the storks the mother explained how the bird had been involved in their creation. The girls listened intently and then one whispered to the other, 'Should we tell her the facts of life or shall we let her remain in ignorance?'

When the baby was due the father-to-be went to the maternity ward and spent an anxious period in the waiting room. Suddenly, a nurse came runnning out shouting, 'Hot water, quick!'
The nervous man rushed forward and said: 'What is it? Is the baby coming?'
'No,' the nurse replied. 'The doctor wants a cup of instant coffee'

As the birth of the baby became imminent the father telephoned the hospital. Unfortunately, he got through to the local cricket club by mistake. 'Has anything happened?' he asked. The man almost fainted when the voice at the other end of the line replied, 'Oh, yes they are all out . . . the last three were ducks!'

When I asked my wife what she wanted for her birthday she said, 'Not to be reminded of it.'

Little Jane missed the sex education lesson at school so she asked her young friend Jamie what it was all about.
Jamie pondered for a moment and then said, 'Oh, it was very simple. All you have to do is cover an egg with some Spam.'

Did you hear about the idiot who was given a pair of water skis for his birthday?

He's spent the last six months looking for a lake with a slope.

The only sure way to remember your wife's birthday is to forget it once.

When a man has a birthday he may take a day off. When a woman has a birthday she takes ten years off.

Youth is a wonderful thing. It's such a pity it's wasted on the young.

Have you noticed how many more twins are born than ever before? I think children are getting afraid of coming into this world alone.

Middle age is when a woman's hair starts turning from grey to black.

A woman stops telling her age as soon as it starts telling on her.

She's so old every time she goes into an antique shop someone tries to buy her.

We call our baby 'Coffee' because he keeps us awake all night.

There were so many candles on her birthday cake, the cake melted.

When he lit all the candles on his birthday cake three people collapsed from the heat.

If she ever told her real age her birthday cake would be a fire hazard.

I never forget my wife's birthday. It's the day after she reminds me of it.

QUOTES

A baby is an alimentary canal with a loud voice at one and and no responsibility at the other.

E. Adamson

Life is what happens to you while you're making other plans.

Robert Balzer

There are two things in this life for which we are never fully prepared. Twins.

John Billings

Anybody who hates children and dogs can't be all bad.

W.C. Fields

When baby's cries grew harder to bear,
I popped him in the Frigidaire.
I never would have done so if
I'd known he'd be frozen stiff.
My wife said 'George, I'm so unhappy,
Our darling's now completely frappé.'

Harry Graham
More Ruthless Rhymes

One of the most obvious facts about grown-ups to a child is that they have forgotten what it is like to be a child.

Randall Jarrell
Third Book of Criticism

There is only one beautiful child in the world, and every mother has it.

Stephen Leacock

I don't know who my grandfather was. I am much more concerned to know what his grandson will be.

Abraham Lincoln

The four stages of man are infancy, childhood, adolescence and obsolesence.

Art Linklater
A Child's Garden Of Misinformation

It takes, not nine months, but sixty years to make a man.

André Malraux

This would be a better world for children if parents had to eat the spinach.

Groucho Marx
Animal Crackers

My mother loved children – she would have given anything if I had been one.

Groucho Marx

A bit of talcum,
Is always walcum.

Ogden Nash
Reflections of Babies

Experience is what enables you to make the same mistake again without getting caught.

Ralph Peterson

The more people have studied different methods of bringing up children the more they have come to the conclusion that what good mothers and fathers instinctively feel like doing for their babies is best after all.

Dr Benjamin Spock
The Commonsense Book of Baby and Child Care

Monday's child is fair of face,
Tuesday's child is full of grace;.
Wednesday's child is full of woe,
Thursday's child has far to go;
Friday's child is loving and giving,
Saturday's child works hard for its living;
and the child that's born on the Sabbath day, is fair
and wise and good and gay.

Traditional

I have found the best way to give advice to your
children is to find out what they want and then
advise them to do it.

Harry S. Truman

Youngsters today have so many luxuries that the
best way to punish your child is to send him to your
room instead of his.

Earl Wilson

Weddings and anniversaries

Unless it is a very formal affair a wedding speech should appear to be impromptu. This does not mean that it should be unprepared. Preparation for informal gatherings is just as important as for any other occasion.

Any jokes or quotes used should not appear forced. It goes back to what was said at the beginning of this book – gear your speech to the occasion and to the audience.

To most people a wedding speech is the only time they will ever get up on their feet to speak in public. If this applies to you keep your speech as simple as possible – it is easier on your nerves!

The most important aspect of any wedding speech – be it by the best man, groom, or drunken guest – is to be sincere.

For more information on the subject of wedding speeches – indeed the whole subject of wedding etiquette – I suggest you read Angela Lansbury's excellent book *Wedding Speeches and Toasts,* published by Ward Lock.

JOKES

They say that there is nothing in the world harder than a diamond. There is . . . paying for it.

Never criticize your wife's faults. Just think – it may have been those little imperfections that prevented her from getting a better husband.

They got married . . . and lived nappily ever after.

It is said that married men live longer than single men. It's not true – it just seems longer.

To some men marriage is a bit like being in a restaurant. You get exactly what you asked for – but as soon as you see what the fellow on the next table has got you wish you had ordered that instead!

Did you hear about the groom who ordered a new suit for his wedding? It wasn't made in time so he sued the tailor for promise of breeches.

Marriage is like a three-ring circus. First there's the engagement ring, next the wedding ring and then the suffer-ring.

My wife and I have a joint bank account. I put the money in and she takes it out.

She married him for better or for worse. It was better for her and worse for him.

We've been happily married for thirty years. She's happy and I'm married.

I asked her father if I could marry her and he said: 'Just leave your name and address and we'll notify you if nothing better comes up.'

Before marriage a man yearns for her. After marriage the 'Y' is silent.

A wife is a woman who'll stick by you in all the troubles you wouldn't have had if you hadn't married her.

When I got married the best man mislaid the ring. Boy, I got an awful fright – and I'm still married to her.

Before we were married I used to catch her in my arms – now I catch her in my pockets.

They say marriage is an institution – but who wants to live in an institution?

Advice to new husband: Whenever you introduce your wife to someone refer to her as your first wife – that should keep her on her toes.

Marriage is a bit like a card game. They start as a pair; he deals her a diamond; she shows a flush and they end up with a full house.

My wife is wonderful. If I get home late she gives me my slippers and pyjamas. And if anything else is handy she gives me that, too.

Marriage is an attempt to change a night owl into a homing pigeon.

Advice to new husband: Remember that although you are now married, your wife still appreciates chocolates and flowers and new clothes. Let her know you haven't forgotten – mention them occasionally.

When we got married my wife didn't have a rag on her back – but she's got plenty of them now.

My wife says that we have only one thing in common. We both love the same man.

I always face up to my troubles like a man – I blame the wife.

Hell hath no fury like the lawyer of a woman scorned.

I never lose my temper but, I must admit, I do mislay it occasionally.

His wife said she wanted an animal fur, so he bought her a donkey jacket.

Nothing surprises a man more than when his wife finds what she wants on her first dive into her handbag.

English is called the mother tongue because father seldom gets the chance to use it.

After twenty five years of marriage my wife and I still agree. When I'm happy, she's happy and when I'm sad, she's sad . . . when I'm out of the house, we are both happy, and when I'm at home we're both sad.

There are two kinds of people at parties – those who want to stay and those who want to go home. Unfortunately, they are usually married to each other.

My wife went to the hairdresser the other day and asked the stylist to give her a beautiful hair-do. The hairdresser took a long look at my wife and said: 'Madam, this is a comb – not a magic wand.'

Women are more irritable than men, probably because men are more irritating.

I'll always remember our twentieth wedding anniversary. On that day the oven exploded and blew us both out of the house. It was the first time we'd been out together for years.

My wife loves sales. Yesterday she went to the local department store and bought three things that were marked down – two dresses and an escalator.

I bought my wife a red trouser-suit but my wife no longer wears it. She was wearing it once in the High Street when she yawned . . . and two people put letters in her mouth.

For months I complained to my wife that she cared more for her house plants than she did for me. I didn't realise that I was becoming a bit of nag until one day my wife was watering her plants and I said, 'There you go again. I think you care more for those plants than you do for me.'
She crossed the room and said sweetly. 'Darling, of course I care for you as much as I care for the plants.' And then she emptied the watering can over me!

Aren't women wonderful? My wife went to the bank to make a withdrawal yesterday and she asked if she could take it from my half of our joint account.

When I proposed she said, 'I may like the simple things in life but that doesn't mean that I want to marry one of them!'

The bride looked stunning – the groom looked stunned.

I recently paid a researcher £200 to dig up our family tree. Now he's asking for another £200 to keep everything quiet.

There are only two ways to avoid alimony. Either stay single or stay married.

Every husband should have a hobby, but don't let your wife find out about her.

My wife's hobby is making things – like mountains out of molehills.

The weaker sex are the stronger sex because of the weakness of the stronger sex for the weaker sex.

I was talking to our next door neighbour when she mentioned that she had given £5 to a tramp that morning. What did your husband have to say about that? I asked. He said thank you. she replied.

QUOTES

A toast to sweethearts. May all sweethearts become married couples and may all married couples remain sweethearts.

Here's to the bride and groom. May their happiness last forever and may we be fortunate enough to continue being part of it.

A successful marriage requires falling in love many times – with the same person.

Every minute you spend being angry with your partner is a waste of sixty seconds in which you could be enjoying your marriage.

Nothing is more responsible for the good old days than a bad memory.

Frank P. Adams

We pondered whether to take a holiday or get a divorce, and we decided that a trip to Bermuda is over in two weeks, but a divorce is something you always have.

Woody Allen

Marriage: The state or condition of a community consisting of a master, a mistress and two slaves, –making in all two.

Ambrose Bierce
The Devil's Dictionary

Rules for a happy married life:
1. Don't nag;
2. Don't try to take your partner over;
3. Don't criticise;
4. Give honest appreciation;
5. Pay little attentions;
6. Be courteous;
7. Read a good book on the sexual side of marriage.

Dale Carnegie
How to Win Friends and Influence People

The women of this country are right good, pleasant, humble, discreet, sober, chaste, obedient to their husbands, true, secret, steadfast, ever busy, never idle, temperate in speaking and virtuous in all their works. Or at least they should be so.

William Caxton
The Dictes and Sayings of the Philosophers

I never married because there was no need. I have three pets at home which serve the same purpose as a husband. I have a dog which growls every morning, a parrot which swears all the afternoon and a cat that comes home late at night.

Marie Corelli

Marriage is not all bed and breakfast.

R. Coulson
Reflections

Once a woman has forgiven her man, she must not reheat his sins for breakfast.

Marlene Dietrich

If you want to know about a man, you can find out an awful lot by looking at who he married.

Kirk Douglas

Husbands are like fires . . . they go out when unattended.

Zsa Zsa Gabor

When one loves somebody everything is clear – where to go, what to do – it all takes care of itself and one doesn't have to ask anybody about anything.

Maxim Gorky
The Zykovs

He (Tarzan) was unaware that he was the lost child of a distinguished explorer and his wife; and when he fell in love with a girl whom he saved from the gangs of savage beasts, a delicate scruple prevented him from marrying her. She could not fathom the reason. Then it came out: 'My mother was an ape.' he said simply!

Robert Graves & Alan Hodge
The Long Week End

The critical period in matrimony is breakfast time.

A.P. Herbert

Marriage has many pains, but celibacy has no pleasures.

Dr Samuel Johnson

The most difficult year of marriage is the one you're in.

Franklin P. Jones

When you're bored with yourself, marry and be bored with someone else.

David Pryce-Jones
Owls and Satyrs

Marrying a man is like buying something you've been admiring in a shop window. You may love it when you get home, but it doesn't always go with everything else in the house.

Jean Kerr
The Snake Has All The Lines

The female of the species is more deadly than the male.

Rudyard Kipling
The Female of the Species

Any man who says he can see through women is missing a lot.

Groucho Marx

The great secret of a successful marriage is to treat all disasters as incidents and none of the incidents as disasters.

Harold Nicholson

I've been married so many times my marriage certificate now reads: 'To whom it may concern.'

Mickey Rooney

A husband is what is left of the lover after the nerve has been extracted.

Helen Rowland
A Guide To Men

I like men to behave like men – strong and childish.
Françoise Sagan

The course of true love never did run smooth.
William Shakespeare
A Midsummer Night's Dream

Men are April when they woo, December when they wed: maids are May when they are maids, but the sky changes when they are wives.
William Shakespeare
As You Like It

Like fingerprints, all marriages are different.
George Bernard Shaw

Marriage is popular because it combines the maximum of temptation with the maximum of opportunity.
George Bernard Shaw

It is a woman's business to get married as soon as possible, and a man's to keep unmarried as long as he can.
George Bernard Shaw

Love is as strong as death.
The Song of Solomon 8:6

Marriage is like life in this – that it is a field of battle, and not a bed of roses.
Robert Louis Stevenson

In the spring a young man's fancy lightly turns to thoughts of love.
Alfred, Lord Tennyson
Locksley Hall

The first duty of love is to listen.
Paul Tillich

Marry on Monday for health.
Tuesday for wealth.
Wednesday for the best day of all.
Thursday for losses.
Friday for crosses.
Saturday no luck at all.

Traditional

Marriage is a bribe to make a housekeeper think she's a householder.

Thornton Wilder
The Matchmaker

The best part of married life is the fights. The rest is merely so-so.

Thornton Wilder
The Matchmaker

At work

Speeches connected with the work place fall into two distinct categories – business and personnel.

Business includes company dinners, sales present-ations and annual meetings.

Personnel covers social affairs such as Christmas parties, birthdays, someone leaving, promotions, and retirement.

As a general rule any speeches relating to business will be more formal, and probably longer, than those that fall into the personnel category.

Many of the jokes and quotes given in the section on birthdays can be usefully adapted for a retire-ment speech.

JOKES

It's finally happened – the deductions have exceeded my salary. Last month the company didn't send me a cheque they sent me a bill.

When I came home from a business trip the other day my wife helped unpack my suitcase. She put away my razor, shaving cream, after-shave, shower talc, mouth wash and aspirin. Then she gave me a big hug and said, 'Darling, it's nice to have you back in the bathroom cabinet.'

Give a man enough rope and he'll get tied up at the office.

Our new secretary can't spell – which makes her inability to type a real asset.

Salaries vary according to viewpoint. The factor that determines whether a wage is small or large is whether you are the employer or the employee.

There ought to be a better way to start the day than by getting up in the morning.

When you are at primary school you are advised that if you want to get a good job you should go to secondary school.

While you are at secondary school you are told that to get a good job you ought to go to university.

You go to university and just prior to graduation someone tells you that for a really good job you need to go for a master's degree.

Eventually you get your master's – only to be told that to be really successful requires a doctorate.

On achieving the doctorate you go looking for a job – but everyone is looking for younger men!

Because of my short-sightedness I almost worked myself to death – I couldn't tell whether the boss was watching me or not so I had to work all the time . . . until I got my new glasses!

The new secretary came into work half an hour late, to be greeted by an angry boss. 'You're late!' he roared, 'This is not good enough.'

'No, I'm not late.' replied the secretary, calmly. 'I took my lunch break early today – on my way to work.'

Thanks to the rising cost of living, you are now starving on the income you once dreamed about.

Office Rules:
1. The managing director is always right.
2. If the managing director is wrong Rule One applies.

Our office efficiency expert walks in his sleep. He says that it is good time and motion practice . . . he can rest and get exercise at the same time.

My boss recently went to his lawyer to make a will. Amongst his wishes was that £10,000 be given to each employee who had worked for him for thirty years.

'But you haven't been in business for thirty years.' said the lawyer.

'No,' my boss replied 'But it's good advertising.'

I don't think it's fair to say British workmen are lazy. Why, only the other day I came across a labourer with two spades in his hand – plus the ace of hearts and a king.

A crisis at work is like sex – as long as you keep talking about it, nothing happens.

I don't mind going to work. I don't mind coming home. It's the bit in between that I don't like.

A friend of mine once applied for a job for which he was eminently qualified but did not get a reply for a while. Then, by chance, he met the Company Chairman whom he had known for some time. When he mentioned his job application the Chairman hired him on the spot.

He moved house to be nearer to the office and worked diligently for three months. Then, one day he received a letter from the company that had been forwarded from his old address. It apologised for the delay in replying to his job application but said that he was not called for interview because he lacked the necessary qualifications.

The funny thing was that the letter was signed by himself!

Have you seen the latest, simplified tax forms?

All they ask is: What do you make? What do you spend? What have you got left? Send it to us!

Did you hear about the gang of building workers who failed in their attempt to climb Mount Everest?

They ran out of scaffolding twenty feet from the top.

I know a secretary who's changed her boss six times in the last six months. But she's on her last lap now.

The boss called in his assistant and shook him warmly by the hand. 'Fred, my man, this new project calls for experience, resourcefulness, quick thinking, imagination and hard work. That's why I asked you to come to see me. I think you should retire!'

Old age is like everything else. To make a success of it you've got to start young.

You can tell you're getting old when you begin to wonder why you once queued in the rain to watch films that you now switch off when they appear on television.

We are sorry you are leaving. You are going to be hard to replace . . . at the wage we've been paying you.

To err is human, but to really foul things up requires a computer.

That secretary is terrible but we can't fire her. She's the only one who understands the filing system.

I was off work yesterday because I was sick – sick of work.

I hold a very responsible job. Anything goes wrong, I'm responsible.

Our computer doesn't actually do anything. We just blame it for everything.

QUOTES

Make three correct guesses consecutively and everyone will regard you as an expert.

Success is never final and failure never fatal. It's courage that counts.

Guard agains the fellow who slaps you on the back. It could be to help you swallow something.

To err is human; to blame it on someone else is more so.

Anybody who isn't pulling his weight is probably pushing his luck.

He who aims at the moon may hit the top of a tree; he who aims at the top of a tree is unlikely to get off the ground.

It's quality that counts, not quantity. A fly lays more eggs than a hen.

He who is carried on another's back does not appreciate how far off the town is.
                                        African Proverb

I don't want to achieve immortality through my work. I want to achieve immortality by not dying.
                                        Woody Allen

Change your dwelling place often, for the sweetness of life consists in variety.

Arabic proverb

On the day of victory no fatigue is felt.

Arabic proverb

Man learns little from success, but much from failure.

Arabic proverb

Not in doing what you like best, in liking what you do is the secret of happiness.

J.M. Barrie

Inspiration is to work every day.

Charles Baudelaire

Leave the beaten track occasionally and dive into the woods. You will be certain to find something you have never seen before.

Alexander Graham Bell

Haste is the mother of imperfection.

Brazilian proverb

Ambition can creep as well as soar.

Edmund Burke

Retirement at sixty-five is ridiculous. When I was sixty-five I still had pimples.

George Burns

To forge a fixed and arbitary rule in terms of years as the limit of a man's usefulness of human service would only be to behead a large portion of the world's intellectual and moral leadership and thereby impoverish mankind.

Nicholas Murray Butler

An expert is one who knows more and more about less and less.

Nicholas Murray Butler

A committee is an animal with four back legs.

John Le Carré
Tinker, Tailor, Soldier, Spy

He that is afraid to shake the dice will never throw a six.

Chinese proverb

The height of success in this world is having one's name written everywhere – except in the telephone directory.

Leo Chiosso

No sweet without sweat.

John Clarke

Of course I believe in luck. How else can you explain the success of the people you detest?

Jean Cocteau

If you really want a job done, give it to a busy, important man. He'll have his secretary do it.

Calvin Coolidge

Our life is frittered away by detail . . . Simplify, simplify.

Henry David Thoreau

By the time a person gets to greener pastures, he can't climb the fence.

Frank Dickson

Nothing great was ever achieved without enthusiasm.

Ralph Waldo Emerson

Hitch your wagon to a star.

Ralph Waldo Emerson

One of the saddest things is that the only thing a man can do for eight hours a day, day after day, is work. You can't eat eight hours a day, nor drink for eight hours a day, nor make love for eight hours.

William Faulkner
Writers at Work

If at first you don't succeed, try, try, a couple of times more. Then quit: there's no sense in making a fool of yourself.

W.C. Fields

The idea that to make a man work you've got to hold gold in front of his eyes is a growth, not an axiom. We've done that for so long that we've forgotten there's any other way.

F. Scott Fitzgerald
This Side of Paradise

Spoon feeding, in the long run, teaches nothing but the shape of the spoon.

E.M. Forster

The brain is a wonderful organ; it starts working the moment you get up in the morning, and does not stop until you get to the office.

Robert Frost

Every horse thinks his own pack the heaviest.

Fuller

To believe a business impossible is the way to make it so.

Fuller

A verbal contract isn't worth the paper it's written on.

Sam Goldwyn

The impossible is often untried.

Jim Goodwin

When work is a pleasure, life is a joy! When work is a duty, life is slavery.

Maxim Gorky
The Lower Depths

A committee is a group of the unwilling, picked from the unfit, to do the unecessary.

Richard Harkness

Tender-handed stroke a nettle, and it stings you for your pains; grasp it like a man of mettle, and it soft as silk remains.

Aaron Hill
Verses Written on a Window

You know you've reached middle age when your weight-lifting consists merely of standing up.

Bob Hope

There are two kinds of discontent in this world; the discontent that works and the discontent that wrings its hands. The first gets what it wants, and the second loses what it had. There is no cure for the first but success, and there is no cure at all for the second.

Elbert Hubbard

An invasion of ideas cannot be resisted.

Victor Hugo

When written in Chinese the word crisis is composed of two characters. One represents danger and the other represents opportunity.

John F. Kennedy

If you can keep your head when all about you are losing theirs, it is just possible that you haven't grasped the situation.

Jean Kerr
Please Don't Eat The Daisies

If you have always done it that way, it is probably wrong.

Charles Kettering

Opportunities are usually disguised as hard work, so most people don't recognise them.

Ann Landers

One has to be seventy before one is full of courage. the young are always half-hearted.

D.H. Lawrence

The aim of all legitimate business is service, for profit, at a risk.

Benjamin C. Leeming
Imagination

Your own resolution to succeed is more important than any other one thing.

Abraham Lincoln

Besides the noble art of getting things done, there is the noble art of leaving things undone. The wisdom of life consists in the elimination of non-essentials.

Lin Yutang

If hard work is the key to success, most people would rather pick the lock.

Claude McDonald

Only a mediocre person is always at his best.

W. Somerset Maugham

If men could regard the events of their own lives with more open minds they would frequently discover that they did not really desire the things they failed to obtain.

André Maurois
The Art of Living

If you don't want to work, you have to work to earn enough money so that you won't have to work.

Ogden Nash

Work expands to fill the time available for its completion.

C. Northcote Parkinson

If anyone has a new idea in this country, there are twice as many people who advocate putting a man with a flag in front of it.

Prince Philip

If a man does only what is required of him, he is a slave. The moment he does more, he is a free man.

A.W. Robertson

Some are born great, some achieve greatness, and some have greatness thrust upon them.

William Shakespeare
Twelfth Night

Happy is the man who can make a living by his hobby.

George Bernard Shaw

He that is over-cautious will accomplish little.

Friedrich Schiller

You must learn to obey before you command.

Solon

There are no gains without pains.

Adlai Stevenson

Have you ever noticed that even the busiest people are never too busy to take the time to tell you how busy they are?

Bob Talbert

There is no deodorant like success.

Elizabeth Taylor

A new broom sweeps clean, but the old one finds the corners.

H.W. Thompson

The person who knows how will always have a job. But the person who knows why will be boss.

Carl Wood

Procrastination is the thief of time.

Edward Young
Night Thoughts

After dinner speaking

A person is invited to give an after dinner speech because he or she is either well known in a particular field, someone of high repute, or renowned for after dinner speaking. To receive such an invitation is an honour that should not be taken lightly.

You should take extra care in the preparation of your speech and make absolutely certain that it runs for the time required, is relevant and entertaining.

As a rule an after dinner speech is longer than any of the other speeches mentioned in this book. But the basic rules of preparation and delivery covered in the introduction still prevail, so if you are in doubt refer back to them.

If you are likely to be called upon as a regular after dinner speaker, or if you decide to take it up as a paying proposition, you will need to keep a fund of anecdotes relative to your chosen subject. If these anecdotes relate to your own personal experiences so much the better.

JOKES

In Moscow, *Pravda* is featuring a special competition for the best political joke. The first prize is twenty years in Siberia.

Two men were watching a Western on television. As the hero rode on horseback towards a cliff edge one man said 'I bet you £50 he goes over the cliff.'

'You're on.' said the other man.

The hero rode on . . . and straight over the cliff.

Being a sportsman the second man handed over the money. The first man looked at it and said, 'You know, I feel a bit guilty about winning this. I've seen the film before.'

'So have I.' said the second man, 'But I didn't think he'd be stupid enough to make the same mistake twice.'

The other day he bought himself a new pair of wellingtons. The next day he took them back for a replacement pair . . . with a longer piece of string between them.

A pilgrim returning from Lourdes tried to smuggle an extra bottle of vodka through the green channel at customs but was stopped.

'What's this?' asked the customs officer.

'It's just a bottle of Holy water.' declared the pilgrim.

The customs officer took a good swig from the bottle, then said, 'It tastes more like vodka to me.'

'Amazing!' said the pilgrim. 'Another miracle!'

A white horse went into a pub and ordered a pint of beer. The barman watched him drink the beer, then said 'Did you know there's a whisky named after you?'

The horse replied, 'What . . . Eric?'

Sir Lancelot rode up to the hamburger stall and ordered a quarter pounder with onions and tomato sauce. He was enjoying this snack when Sir Gerwain arrived and ordered a cheeseburger with fries. 'I'm sorry,' said the stallholder but I can't serve you. 'Why not?' asked Sir Gerwain. 'Because' replied the stallholder, 'This is a one knight stand.'

A miser was at the top of a ladder when a coin fell from his pocket. He was hit on the head by the coin as it reached the ground.

Thank you for that kind introduction. I feel that I shall now have to say two prayers for forgiveness: the first for my introducer, because he had told so many lies in praising me so; the second for myself for enjoying it so much.

One of the waitresses has just told me that she has had two improper suggestions made to her tonight and she is rather upset about it. Normally she has about a dozen.

At the race track last week a bookie expressed great surprise when a horse walked up and put a bet on himself. 'What's the matter?' asked the horse, 'Are you amazed to hear a horse speak?' 'No,' the bookie replied, 'I'm surprised that you think you will win.'

I went on a new automatic aeroplane the other day. When we had taken our seats an automatic announcement welcomed us aboard. 'Ladies and gentlemen, welcome to our fully automated aeroplane. It has no pilot and no crew. Press a button and we take off, press another and refreshments are served. Press another and we land. Absolutely nothing can go wrong . . . can go wrong . . . can go wrong . . . can go wrong . . .'

A duck went into the local job centre and said he was looking for a job. 'That's amazing.' said the clerk, 'A duck that can talk!' 'Of course, I can talk.'

said the duck. 'Now stop fooling around and see if you can get me a job.'

As soon as the duck left the clerk telephoned the local circus owner. 'I've just met a talking duck that is looking for a job.'

'A talking duck?' said the circus owner. 'I'll certainly give him a job. Tell him I'll pay him £1,000 a week and all the food he can eat if he'll work in my circus.'

The following day the duck returned to the job centre to be greeted by the enthusing clerk. 'I've found you a marvellous job with the local circus. They'll pay you £1,000 a week and all the food you can eat.'

'Don't be silly.' said the duck. 'That's no good to me, I'm an engineer!'

Did you hear about the stupid woman who decided to iron her curtains?
She fell out of the window.

The other day I visited the local zoo where I saw a rather tipsy gentleman staggering around. When he saw the hippopotamus looking at him he apologised: 'Don't look at me like that, my sweet. I can explain everything.'

I was presenting prizes at a school speech day recently and I tried to say something more orignal than the usual, 'Well done' to each recipient.
Unfortunately I slipped up a little when one very attractive sixteen-year-old girl came up. 'What are you going to do when you leave school?' I asked.
She looked at me, knowingly, and replied 'Well, I was thinking of going straight home.'

Most speakers have four speeches: what they have

prepared, what they actually say, what they wish they had said, and what they are quoted as saying.

Advice for speakers: If you don't strike oil in the first two minutes you'd better stop boring.

Dolphins are so intelligent that within only a few weeks they can train a man to stand on the side of a pool and throw fish to them.

At an exclusive banquet the gourmet heard reference to a fabulous dish called Poy. He enquired about this dish but it turned out that the speaker had only heard of it and had never had the pleasure of tasting the delicacy.

The gourmet was determined to track down this marvellous meal and spent many hours consulting his books – but to no avail. One day he mentioned his quest to another gourmet. This gentleman had not tried the dish but had heard a that it came from a remote village high up in the Himalayas.

Without delay the gourmet set off in search of the illusive Poy. Many months later he arrived at the remote Himalayan village and found the monk who was famous for making Poy.

The monk was quite surprised at the gourmet's attention. 'It's amazing you have never heard of it before as I was given the recipe by a man from London.' he said. 'But, as you have travelled so far I will gladly make Poy just for you. What would you like, Steak and Kidney Poy or Shepherd's Poy?

A friend of mine was caught speeding last week. 'Do you realise, sir, that you were doing seventy five miles an hour?' said the policeman. 'Yes.' replied my friend 'But couldn't you make it ninety? I'm trying to sell this car.'

Last week I arranged to meet a business colleague at a local antiques auction. When I got there I discovered they were auctioning Victorian chamber pots in which I am quite interested. Then I saw my friend on the other side of the room so, naturally, I waved.

'Excuse me, Sir.' said the auctioneer 'But are you bidding?'

'No,' I replied, 'I was just waving to a friend.' Shortly afterwards a chamber pot I rather liked came under the hammer and I decided to bid for it. As soon as I did so the auctioneer took one look at me and said, 'And what is it this time, Sir? Friend or po?'

When the first astronaut landed on a distant planet he found it was populated by beautiful blonde girls. The girls were enthralled by the astronaut's visit and wanted to do everything they could to make his stay as pleasant as possible. This pleased the astronaut immensely but there was just one snag – the girls were all ten feet tall. In desperation he looked through his instruction book and there he found the answer to his dilemma. He walked up to the tallest girl and said boldly 'Take me to your ladder.'

A health fanatic was talking to a group of people.

'I found that the best start to the day is to exercise for a while, take several deep breaths and have a cold shower. Then I feel rosy all over.'

At that point there came a request from the back of the room. 'Tell us more about Rosie.'

Did you hear about that new organisation Teetotallers Anonymous? If you feel like going on the wagon, you call this number and two drunks come round to talk to you.

A teacher in a Moscow school asked one of his pupils to name the five biggest Russian traitors. The boy replied: 'Trotsky, Stalin, Malenkov, Kruschev and Yeltsin.' The teacher went red in the face and dragged the child out into the school corridor and demanded: 'OK, wiseguy. Who gave you next year's answers?'

Did you hear about the tycoon who had a heart attack in his office. As his secretary rushed into the office he said: 'Don't just stand there. Go out and buy a hospital.'

'Why is it you never play golf with Freddie Farsnbarn any more?' asked Charlie's wife. 'Would you play with someone who cheats with his own scorecard, moves his ball when the other player isn't looking, has a tantrum when he loses and then gets drunk in the bar after the game?' said Charlie. 'No.' replied his wife. 'Well.' said Charlie 'Neither will he.'

QUOTES

Sometimes the difference between a good speaker and a poor speaker is a comfortable nap.

O.A. Battista

Give me my golf clubs, the fresh air, and a beautiful girl for a partner, and you can keep my golf clubs and the fresh air.

Jack Benny

An after-dinner speech should be like a lady's dress – long enough to cover the subject and short enough to be interesting.

R.A. Butler

The best cure for drunkenness is while sober to see a drunken man.

Chinese proverb

If you actually look like your passport photo, you aren't well enough to travel.

Sir Vivian Fuchs

Humour cannot be learnt. Besides wit and keeness of mind, it presupposes a large measure of goodness of heart, of patience, of tolerance and of human kindness.

Curt Goetz

Life is like a sewer. What you get out of it depends on what you put in to it.

Tom Lehrer
We Will All Go Together When We Go

We may live without poetry, music and art;
We may live without conscience and live without heart;
We may live without friends; we may live without books;
But civilised man cannot live without cooks.

Lord Lytton

The art of public life consists to a great extent of knowing exactly where to stop and going a bit further.

H.H. Munro

The ideal man is healthy and fit and has a well-trained mind. The bookworm and the gladiator are only half-trained men, leading only half a life.

Prince Philip

Champagne and orange juice is a great drink. The orange improves the champagne. The champagne definitely improves the orange.

Prince Philip

Do all the good you can,
By all the means you can,
In all the ways you can,
In all the places you can,
At all the times you can,
To all the people you can,
As long as ever you can.

John Wesley

It is only about things that do not interest one that one can give a really unbiased opinion, which is no doubt the reason why an unbiased opinion is always valueless.

Oscar Wilde

All occasions

The following jokes and quotes may be found useful for a wide variety of speeches.

JOKES

Argument
If you want the last word in an argument say, 'I expect you are right.'

Blotting Paper
Something you search for while the ink dries.

Cigarettes
I decided to give up cigarettes in two stages. First I'm going to give up smoking my cigarettes . . . and then I'll give up smoking other people's.

Driving
If your wife wants to learn to drive, don't stand in her way.

Economist
One who knows how to throw the money he hasn't got after the money he never had.

A man who tells you what to do with your money after you've done something else with it.

Economy
Going without something you want in case you

should sometime want something you probably don't want.

Something you should practise if you had something left you could practise with.

A form of thrift that's easier to practise when you're broke.

Education
Something which enables you to pass out insults and call it repartee.

What is left after you have forgotten everything you have been taught.

Efficiency Expert
A man who kills two birds with one stone – and gets the stone back.

A man who waits to make up a foursome before going through a revolving door.

Egotist
One the nicest things about an egotist is that he never talks about other people.

I wouldn't say he's conceited – but with the whole world to fall in love with, he chose himself.

Estate Agents
Estate agents have two types of house: the ones you don't want and the ones you can't afford.

Feminine Instinct
The instinct that tells a woman she is right – whether she is or not.

Gentleman
A true gentleman is a man who knows how to play the bagpipes – but doesn't.

Glove
Something that keeps one hand warm while you look for its mate.

Hangover
Today is one of those days because last night was one of those nights.

Home Cooking
Where many a man thinks his wife is.

Jogging
Jogging can really increase your body awareness. I've now got aching muscles in places where I never knew I had muscles.

Jogging is great for losing weight. I now buy my jogging shorts in three sizes – May, July and September.

The trouble with jogging is that by the time you realize you are not fit enough to do it, you've got a long walk home.

Luck
I'm so unlucky that if ever my ship comes in there will probably be a dock strike on.

Money
Always borrow money from a pessimist. He won't expect to get it back.

These days birds are the only creatures to have nest eggs.

Narrow Mindedness
He is so narrow minded he can look through a keyhole with both eyes at the same time.

Rarity
There is nothing so rare as a juggernaut driver with an inferiority complex.

Self-Defence
The first lesson in the art of self defence is to keep your glasses on.

Speed
Every time I start thinking that the world is moving too fast, I go to the Post Office.

Surprise
I love surprises as long as I'm ready for them.

Telephone
Have you ever noticed that wrong numbers are never busy?

Will
My aunt had a cat and a parrot. When she died she left all of her estate to the cat. Now the parrot is contesting the will.

QUOTES

Ability
No-one knows what he can do till he tries.

Publilius Syrus

Abusiveness
Keep raising the roof and people will think there's something wrong in your attic.

Franklin P. Jones

Advice
A knife of the keenest steel requires the whetstone, and the wisest man needs advice.

Zoroaster

Agreeability
My idea of an agreeable person is a person who agrees with me.

Benjamin Disraeli

Aim in Life
An aim in life is the only fortune worth finding.

Robert Louis Stevenson

Antagonist
He that wrestles with us strengthens our nerves and sharpens our skill. Our antagonist is our helper.

Edmund Burke

Argument
The second blow makes the fray.

Francis Bacon

If you argue and rankle and contradict, you may achieve a victory sometimes; but it will be an empty victory because you will never get your opponent's goodwill.

Benjamin Franklin

Beauty
A thing of beauty is a joy forever.

John Keats
Endymion

Blind
If the blind lead the blind, both shall fall into the ditch.

Matthew 15:14

Bore
A healthy male adult bore consumes each year one and a half times his own weight in other people's patience.

John Updike
Confessions of a Wild Bore

Brain
My brain; it's my second favourite organ.

Woody Allen

If the human brain was simple enough for us to understand we'd be so simple we couldn't.

Chance
Blind and rash is he who lets chance lead him.

Seneca

Cheerfulness
Cheerfulness in doing renders a deed more acceptable.

Fuller

Church
The Absentee's Alphabet
I'd like to go to church but . . .
A is for Auntie, who will come to tea,
B is for Bed, which won't release me
C is for Car, 'We need the fresh air',
D is for Dinner Mum must prepare
E is for Enthusiasm, which I haven't got
F is for Foursome, which golf's quite a lot
G is for Garden, much 'nearer God's heart'
H is for Husband, who won't play his part.
I is for Intruders who sit in my pew
J is for Jealousy shown by a few
K is for Knitting which Mum likes so much
L is for Language, it's so out of touch
M is for Money, they always want more
N is for New tunes we've not heard before
O is for Overtime, double on Sunday
P is for Preparing I must do for Monday
Q is for Queer noises which come from the choir
R is for Rector, he ought to retire
S is for Sermons, as dull as can be
T is for Telly I really must see
U is for Unfriendliness I always find
V is for Voices of the women behind
W is for Weather, too much rain or snow
Y is for Young rowdies, who sit at the back
Z is for Zeal – and that's what I lack.

Cleverness
It is great cleverness to know how to conceal one's cleverness.

La Rochefoucauld

Comfort
Words of comfort, skilfully administered, are the oldest therapy known to man.

Louis Nizer

Complaints
Don't complain about the snow on your neighbour's roof when your own doorstep is unclean.

Confucius

Confidence
Confidence is simply that quiet, assured feeling you have just before you fall flat on your face.

Dr L. Binder

Contentment
Contentment is often the result of being too lazy to kick.

Criticism
It is easier to tear down than to build up.

French proverb

Nobody wants constructive criticism. It's all we can do to put up with constructive praise.

Mignon McLaughlin

Pay no attention to what the critics say. A statue has never been erected in honour of a critic.

Jean Sibelius

Curiosity
Curiosity may have killed the cat, but where human beings are concerned, the only thing a healthy curiosity can kill is ignorance.

Harry Lorayne
Secrets of Mind Power

Deceit
Oh what a tangled web we weave, when first we practise to deceive.

Walter Scott
Marmion

Depression
If you feel down just consider that the sun sinks every night – but it rises again in the morning.

Dislike
When a man is not liked, whatever he does is amiss.

Fuller

Doctors
Doctors are lucky. the sun sees their successes – the earth covers their mistakes.

Greek saying

Doubts
Give me the benefit of your convictions, if you have any; but keep your doubts to yourself, for I have enough of my own.

Johann von Goethe

Dreams
There are no rules of architecture for a castle in the clouds.

G.K. Chesterton

Envy
Envy is an admission of inferiority.

Victor Hugo

Expectation
Blessed is he who expects nothing, for he shall
never be disappointed.

Alexander Pope

Family Skeleton
If you cannot get rid of the family skeleton, you
may as well make it dance.

George Bernard Shaw

Fanatic
A fanatic is one who can't change his mind and
won't change the subject.

Winston Churchill

Feelings
You cannot make yourself feel something you do
not feel, but you can make yourself do right in spite
of your feelings.

Pearl S. Buck

Fool
Only a fool tests the depth of the water with both
feet.

African proverb

Everyone is a damn fool for at least five minutes every
day. Wisdom is not exceeding the limit.

Elbert Hubbard

Forgiveness
The more a man knows the more he forgives.

Catherine the Great

Forgiveness needs to be accepted, as well as
offered, before it is complete.

C.S. Lewis

Free Speech
No nation is so poor that it cannot afford free speech.

Daniel Moynihan

There's a big difference between free speech and cheap talk.

Friction
Friction reveals truths that reality obscures.

Jessamyn West

Friendliness
Some folks make you feel at home. Others make you wish you were.

Arnold Glasgow

Genius
Sometimes men come by the name of genius in the same way an insect comes by the name of centipede – not because it has a hundred feet, but because most people can't count above fourteen.

George Lichtenberg

Goodness
Goodness is easier to recognise than to define.

W.H. Auden

Greatness
A great man shows his greatness by the way he treats little men.

Thomas Carlyle

There is a great man who makes every man feel small. But the real great man is the man who makes every man feel great.

Charles Dickens

Greed
There is a sufficiency in the world for man's need but not for man's greed.

Mahatma Gandhi

Hatred
Hatred is never ended by hatred, but by love.

Buddha

Health
If a man thinks about his health he inevitably comes to the conclusion that he is ill.

Honesty
Honest is the cat when the milk's away.

Cheales

The best measurement of a man's honesty isn't his income tax return. It's the zero adjustment on his bathroom scales.

Arthur C. Clarke

Humour
Everything is funny as long as it is happening to somebody else.

Will Rogers

Impressions
If you would stand well with a great mind, leave him with a favourable impression of yourself; if with a little mind, leave him with a favourable impression of himself.

Samuel Taylor Coleridge

Interest
When you ask from a stranger that which is of interest only to yourself, always enclose a stamp.

Abraham Lincoln

Journey
A journey of a thousand miles must begin with a single step.

Lao-Tze

Kindness
The whole worth of a kind deed lies in the love that inspires it.

The Talmud

One of the most difficult things to give away is kindness – it is usually returned.

Letters
One of the pleasures of reading old letters is the knowledge that they need no answer.

Lord Byron

Lie
It is easier to believe a lie that one has heard a thousand times than to believe a fact that one has never heard before.

Robert Lynd

Life
Life can't be all bad when for a few pounds you can buy all the Beethoven sonatas and listen to them for ten years.

William Buckley

Listening
To entertain some people all you have to do is listen.

Losing
The only time losing is more fun than winning is when you're fighting temptation.

Tom Wilson

Memory
Memory is the diary we all carry about with us.

Oscar Wilde

Misfortune
Misfortune arrives on horseback but departs on foot.

Mishaps
Mishaps are like knives that either serve us or cut us as we grasp them by the blade or the handle.

James Russell Lowell

Monarchy
The monarchy is the oldest profession in the world.

Prince Charles

Money
What is not needed is dear at a farthing.

Cato

There is no fortress so strong that money cannot take it.

Cicero

Money makes money and the money money makes makes money.

Benjamin Franklin

Whatever you have, spend less.

Johnson

Music
Where words fail, music speaks.

Hans Christian Andersen

He who sings scares away his woes.

Miguel Cervantes

Music is the universal language of mankind.

Henry Wadsworth Longfellow
Outre Mer

Naturalness
Nothing prevents us from being natural so much as the desire to appear so.

La Rochefoucauld

Negotiations
When you go to buy, don't show your silver.

Chinese proverb

Nude Dancing
The trouble with nude dancing is that not everything stops when the music stops.

Sir Robert Helpmann

Optimism
I am an optimist. But I'm an optimist who takes his raincoat.

Sir Harold Wilson

Patience
In any contest between power and patience, bet on patience.

W.B. Prescott

Position
It's always easy to tell your station in life. Sooner or later someone tells you where to get off.

Herb Daniels

Positive Thinking
They can because they think they can.

Virgil

Praise
Let another man praise thee and not thine own mouth.

Old Testament

Prayer
Even the prayers of an ant reach to heaven.

Japanese proverb

Problems
When a situation cannot be altered, don't waste energy being dissatisfied.

Dr Theodore R. van Dellen

Procrastination
Look before you leap is an excellent maxim. But do not make the mistake of looking for too long, or you will never leap.

Progress
Be not afraid of going slowly, only of standing still.

Chinese proverb

Promises
Promises and pie crust are made to be broken.

Jonathan Swift

Proof
'For example' is not proof.

Jewish proverb

Rain
When the heavens weep, the earth shall live.

Hawaiian proverb

Reading
To read without reflecting is like eating without digesting.

Edmund Burke

Right
Being in the right does not depend on having a loud voice.

Chinese proverb

Second Thoughts
If second thoughts came before first thoughts how much wiser would we be.

Serving Men
I had six honest serving men,
They taught me all I knew;
Their names were Where and What and When
and Why and How and Who.

Rudyard Kipling

Silence
Silence is one great art of conversation.

William Hazlitt

Silence never makes mistakes.

Hindu proverb

A closed mouth gathers no foot.

Silence is not always golden – sometimes it's guilt.

Skill
Skill to do comes of doing.

Emerson

Sneeze
The Autocrat of Russia possesses more power than any other man in the earth; but he cannot stop a sneeze.

Mark Twain

Sore Throat
I have a perfect cure for a sore throat – cut it.

Alfred Hitchcock

Success
Success is the child of audacity.

Benjamin Disraeli

Temper
Temper, if ungoverned, governs the whole man.

Anthony Shaftesbury

Temptation
It's always hard to fight temptation. There is always the nagging thought that it might not happen again.

Travel
A man should know something of his own country, too, before he goes abroad.

Lawrence Stern

In making up a party for a travelling excursion, always be sure to include one ignorant person who will ask all the questions you are ashamed to ask, and you will acquire a great deal of information you would otherwise lose.

Charles Dudley Warner

Trumpet
Get someone else to blow your trumpet and the sound will carry twice as far.

Will Rogers

Truth
Men occasionally stumble over the truth, but most of them pick themselves up and hurry off as if nothing had happened.

Winston Churchill

Wants
As long as I have a want, I have a reason for living. Satisfaction is death.

George Bernard Shaw

Wisdom
Wisdom is knowledge tempered with judgement.

Lord Ritchie-Calder

Women
Women and sparrows twitter in company.

Japanese proverb

Wonders
The world will never starve for want of wonders; but only for want of wonder.

G.K. Chesterton

Words
I would never use a long word when a short word would answer the purpose.

Holmes

Worry
Blessed in the person who is too busy to worry in the daytime, and too sleepy to worry at night.

Leo Aikman

Yesterday
Don't let yesterday take up too much of today.

Will Rogers

Deft definitions

Definitions are very useful for inserting a little light relief into a speech.

I have been collecting them from various sources ever since I was a teenager. What follows is just a small selection from my collection, which I hope you will be able to use.

Abstinence
The thin edge of the pledge.

Absurdity
A statement of belief inconsistent with one's own opinion.

Acquaintance
Someone you know well enough to borrow from, but not well enough to lend to.

Adolescence
When a girl begins to powder and a boy begins to puff.

Adolescent
A teenager who acts like a baby when you don't treat him like an adult.

Advertising
The art of arresting human intelligence long enough to get money from it.

Anatomy
Something everybody has – but it looks better on a girl.

Appetisers
Little things you keep eating until you've lost your appetite.

Bachelor
A man with no ties – except those that need washing.

A man who has faults he doesn't know about yet.

Bank
A place that will lend you money if you can prove you don't need it.

Beach
A place where people slap you on the back and ask how you're peeling.

A place where a woman goes when she's got nothing to wear.

Beauty
What a woman has when she looks the same after washing her face.

Bigamist
A man who's taken one too many.

A man who leads a double wife.

Bore
Someone who talks when you want him to listen.

Someone who is here today, and here tomorrow.

Bottle
A container used for bringing up babies and bringing down adults.

Boxer
A man who hurts the one he gloves.

Bridge
A game of cards in which a good deal depends upon a good deal.

Bus
A vehicle that runs faster when you're after it than it does when you're in it.

Careful Driver
One who has just spotted the police speed trap.

Coincide
What you do when it starts raining.

Collision
When two motorists go after the same pedestrian.

Congratulation
Sugar coated envy.

Conscience
Something that makes you tell your wife before somebody else does.

Cough
Something you yourself can't help but which everyone else does to annoy you.

Courage
The art of being the only one who knows you're scared to death.

Credit Card
What you use to buy today what you can't afford tomorrow while you're still paying for it yesterday.

Critic
Someone who is quick on the flaw.

Someone who goes along for deride.

Criticism
Something you can avoid by saying nothing, doing nothing, and being nothing.

Croquette
A romantic female frog.

Culture
A thin veneer easily soluble in alcohol.

Cynic
A man who looks down on people above him.

A man who regards getting engaged as a first step towards a divorce.

Dancing
The art of pulling your feet away faster than your partner can step on them.

Desk
A waste-paper basket with drawers.

Diagnosis
Inside information.

Doctor
The only man who enjoys poor health.

Dream Girl
One who costs twice as much as you dreamed she would.

Drip
Someone you can always hear, but never turn off.

Drunk
A person who drinks like a fish, but who would be better off if he drank only what a fish does.

Duty
Something one looks forward to without pleasure, does with reluctance, and boasts about afterwards.

Egotist
One who is always me deep in conversation.

Escalator
Stairway to the stores.

Expert
One who takes a subject you already know and makes it sound confusing.

Fashion
Something which goes out of style as soon as everyone has one.

Something which goes in one year and out the other.

Feminine Instinct
The instinct that tells a woman she is right – whether she is or not.

Free Speech
Using someone else's telephone.

Fungi
The life and soul of the party.

Garden
Something most men prefer to turn over in their minds.

Genius
Someone who shoots at something that no-one else can see, and hits it.

Girdle
The difference between fact and figure.

Golf
A long walk punctuated with disappointments.

Gossip
Something that runs down more people than cars.

Letting the chat out of the bag.

Harp
A naked piano.

Hollywood
A place where a woman takes a man for better for worse but not for keeps.

Home
Place where a man can say what he likes – because no-one takes any notice of him anyway.

Honeymoon
The short period between 'I do' and 'You'd better'.

Horsepower
Something that was much safer when only horses had it.

Housework
Something a woman does but which no-one notices – until she doesn't do it.

Hypochondriac
Someone who enjoys pill health.

Impossible
Something that nobody can do – until somebody does it.

Inflation
A way of cutting a five pound note in half without damaging the paper.

Influence
Something you think you have until you try to use it.

Insurance
Something that keeps you poor all your life so that you can die rich.

Intermittent
A romantic proposal when camping.

Intuition
The amazing sense that enables a woman to contradict her husband before he even says anything.

Joint Account
Something that is never overdrawn by the wife, just under-deposited by the husband.

Jury
Twelve people who determine which side has the best lawyer.

Kiss
The greatest substitute for an alibi.

Leadership
The art of getting someone else to do something you want done because he wants to do it.

Lollypop
A sugar daddy.

Motorist
Someone who keeps pedestrians in good running order.

Necessity
A luxury that you bought on hire purchase.

Nudist
Someone who suffers from clothestrophobia.

Nudist Camp
A place where men and women air their differences.

Nursery School
A place where they teach those who hit, not to hit –
and those that don't hit, to hit back.

Pedestrian
Someone who was certain there was petrol in the
tank even though the gauge registered empty.

Perfect Man
The one your wife could have married.

Police Helicopter
A whirlybird that catches the worm.

Prune
A plum that worried a lot.

Punctuality
The art of assessing how late the other person is
going to be.

Race Horse
The only creature that can take thousands of people
for a ride at the same time.

Reality
A delusion created by an alcohol deficiency.

Recession
A period when we have to go without things our grandparents never heard of.

Rhumba
Waving goodbye without using your hands.

Riding
The art of keeping the horse between you and the ground.

Road Map
Something that tells a motorist everything he wants to know – except how to fold it up again.

Scandal
Something that has to be bad to be good.

School
Place where kids go to catch colds from each other so they can stay at home.

Sneeze
Much achoo about nothing.

Solicitor
A man who makes sure that you get what's coming to him.

Sore Throat
Hoarse and buggy.

Split Second
The time between the lights changing and the driver behind you honking his horn.

Tact
The ability to describe others as they see themselves.

Taxpayer
The cross section of the public.

Television
An electric device which, when broken, stimulates conversation.

Towel
One of those little things sent to dry us.

Vegetarian
Someone who is nice to meat.

Vice Versa
Poetry that is not suitable for children.

Wife
Someone who can't see a garage door at ten yards – but who can spot a blonde hair on her husband's jacket half a mile away.

Will Power
The ability to eat just one salted peanut.

Subject Index

Who Said It?

Whilst every effort has been made to identify the source of the quotations given, this has not proved possible in every case.

ALSO IN THE WORK MATTERS SERIES

CVs and Written Applications 0 7063 7272 7
Interviews: How To Succeed 0 7063 7271 9

THE FAMILY MATTERS SERIES

Aromatherapy 0 7063 7227 1
The Bridegroom's Handbook 0 7063 7226 3
Card Games 0 7063 7225 5
Card Games for One 0 7063 7224 7
Card Games for Two 0 7063 7223 9
Chinese Horoscopes 0 7063 7222 0
The Complete Wedding Handbook 0 7063 7217 4
How to be the Best Man 0 7063 7219 0
Wedding Etiquette 0 7063 7220 4
Wedding Speeches and Toasts 0 7063 7218 2